What Lies Within

What Lies Within

SARA TRIPATHI

PAPER TOWNS
PUBLISHERS

PAPER TOWNS
PUBLISHERS

First published by
Papertowns Publishers
72, Vishwanath Dham Colony,
Niwaru Road, Jhotwara,
Jaipur, 302012

What Lies Within

ISBN Print Book - 978-81-951287-2-3

Cover Design by Aditi Shah
Instagram Id: @the.book.story
aditicshah01@gmail.com

Acknowledgements

I stared at the blinking cursor for a whole of 48 minutes before starting to write these acknowledgements. There is just so much to say, so much to be grateful for, so many people to thank, that I didn't even know where to start, so I just sat here completely overwhelmed staring at a blank page. Before I start with anything, I just want to say that there will be so much left unsaid, and so much/many I couldn't mention here and I'm sorry for that. First things first, this is for my parents, family, friends and my teacher who is also my mentor; all of you are my backbone, my spine and my whole being would collapse without you all.

This is for my grandparents, nani-nana I am who I am because of you both; you are the very foundation of my being, my very strength I wouldn't be here if it weren't for your undying support and tremendous encouragement. There aren't enough words in English language, in fact any language that can express how thankful and grateful I am to have two super heroes like you both in my life. Nani you're the most brave, powerful and honest person I will ever come across in life and it is because of women like you that I have steel for a spine. Nana you're support for anything and everything keeps me going, you taught me patience and how much power it holds. I love you both with every cell, every atom of my being.

To my parents, mom-dad, how do I even thank you both for everything you have ever done for me, it's quite literally impossible and I might be good with words but nobody's that good with words. I have absolutely no idea where to begin and where to end; a simple thank you wouldn't suffice. But that's all I've got, so thank you for being the best parents out there and thank you for supporting my extremely ambitious dreams. Pa you taught me perseverance and honesty better than any book or any life lesson could ever do, and there is no one out there I look up to more than you, you're my ideal and I wouldn't want it any other way. Mamma you taught me to thrive and to never give up on things I want, thank you for being the most open and accepting and understanding mother there is out there. I love you both endlessly.

To my brother, "I" thank you for reading every unedited, full of mistakes, piece I ever wrote. You complained a little and whined a little but in the end were always there, thank you for understanding my typos and errors when I couldn't even understand my typos and errors. Thank you for everything, I love you more than I love coffee. To my teacher, Mrs. Annie Mathew, if it weren't for you I probably would've given up on writing long ago, you gave me the gentle push when I needed it and words of encouragement when I was down. A lifetime isn't enough to hold the amount of gratitude I have for you, you mentored me and you supported me, and it is your undying support and love that I am here, no words are enough to thank you.

To my friends, Kavya thank you for forever being my anchor, and reading my pieces before anyone even knew I had a hunch for writing, thank you for your support and a gazillion good memories, cheers to short attendance and weirdness, you're your favorite poet's favorite person, I love you, you know I do. To Jyotika, there is nobody out there who has hyped me up more than you have, and there is nobody out here who will hype me up more than you do, cheers to one direction and ted talks, I love you. To Sanskriti, thank you for always reading what I wrote, even the most trivial and mundane things, and thank you for always being honest, thank you for tolerating me, I know I'm annoying and obnoxious at times. Cheers to fictional characters and never running out of things to talk about, I love you. To Kriti,

Krits I couldn't be more grateful to have you in my life, thank you for existing and tolerating my annoying self and thank you for always being there. Cheers to books and coffee and music, I love you.

To Abhi, thank you for always being just one call away, and thank you for being honest and supportive. Thank you for sitting on the steps with me and helping me edit and most of all thank you for believing in me. I love you.

Lastly, I would like to thank everyone from the Bookoholics and Paper Towns team who made this book come true, if it weren't for you all this book would have just remained a dream. I would like to thank my project managers, Mr. Narendra Singh and Ms. Khyati Gehlot for handling this project so dedicatedly, my editor Ms. Chandani Soni for correcting all my typos and errors and making this book comprehensible, my cover designer Ms. Aditi for giving me the most perfect cover for my book and everyone else who was involved in the different processes of making this book reach shelves.

One of the most revolutionary writers in the world of classic literature, Jane Austen quoted in one of her many great books:

> *"But people themselves alter so much, that there is something new to be observed in them forever."*
>
> *–Jane Austen, Pride and Prejudice.*

These poems are a journey of how I altered, how I changed and how I let hope finally in again. I put across an ocean, a world and a galaxy; I altered, for you to read and realise that you are not alone in this fight. These are my words, and my heart laid bare, for you to see and read and understand that everyone fights a million battles inside, but not everyone's story comes to life. These are poems about hate, anger, wars and destruction, but also about how you plant a seed of hope, and you wait and wait as if it will never grow, but it grows and enters your life, like that morning light enters your room through the blinds, subtle and soft, yet making everything glow in its wake. These phrases are about self-hate turned self-love, and how you find happiness in places you never thought you would.

Come home, the dark seems never-ending, I know, but morning always comes no matter what, so come home, to warmth and to yourself. Let's sweep the darkness under our beds; so just come home. This is my journey and how much I've lost, but I lost things only to gain some more, this is my story, and how darkness consumed me whole and I vowed never to risk hope, but then I did, and I let it grow, and I found myself in the midst of this chaos, I came home to peace and more.

PART ONE

Of the darkness,
And the Cries.

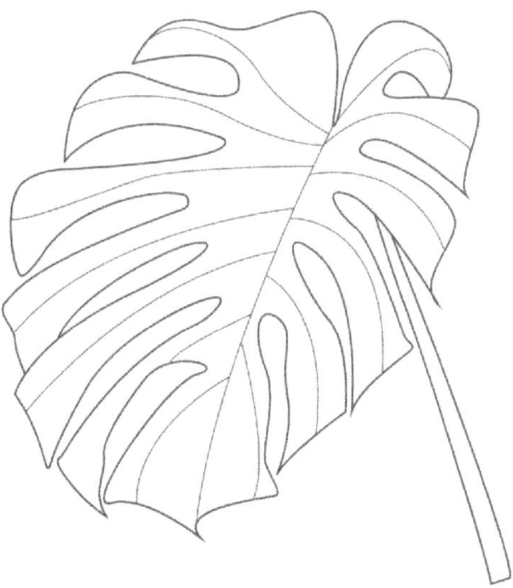

The spiral of suffering

The down side of the city, no one really goes there.
There are trees and moss and dirt and all things unwanted,
With signs of buildings which were once whole, and alive.
Now no more than just ruins.

Ruins. Calls it the world. Collateral damage I call it.
Damage of change and abandonment and destruction.
Damage of us, by us.
That part of the city is abandoned and terrifying
but it's fascinating just the same.

I look at the houses with roofs collapsed and
Doors hanging by their hinges;
And windows barely there,
Just big holes in the walls and the plaster
And paint peeling off.
No sign of life, yet the memories of a hundred lived.

What are these houses, a statement,
A sign of how tragedy unwinds,
once alive now dead and beyond,
What are these houses?
Their remnants, a souvenir to be taken,
a picture to be painted of sufferings
and terrible things that one accounts.

I saw a toy or more like remnants of it,
signs of childhood memories that no longer fit,
I saw a mirror broken to pieces, and a photo frame shattered
beyond repair,
just like the lives that faced despair.

This is proof that nothing lasts,
not your mortal body or the things aghast.
Not the things you buy or the things you steal,
the end will always come as real as you feel.
What will be left will just be a broken piece of a life once
lived,
The pieces left for the coming to see.

We suffer and we not,
We dance and we fix,
We laugh and we love,
We give and we take,
We steal and we borrow,
We breathe and we exhale,
We pass beliefs and religion from generation to generation,
We hope that we will be remembered,
We hope to be not just the speck in the spectrum.
We hope to bring significance,
Yet in the end,
We live and then we perish.
But the suffering never ends.

Melodies inside the head

Instrument of my life, over spilling like fine wine,
brimming with secrets, sublime. Where love, trust and
mystery binds.

I speak a lot, I always have, always something to say.
Relevant - irrelevant, sane - insane, I talk and talk and talk.
Sometimes I make sense other times I don't,
because you see this head of mine thrums to beats of its own.

When I can't speak, I write, because how else will I suffice,
every speck that makes an appearance in my mind.
I've been called strange my whole life,
but don't the strangest things always go up for an extravagant price.

Overspilling, like fine linen,
Putting covers on meaningful things, crying over sins.
Writing, reading, breaking down, breaking through,
an abundance of incomplete brew.
This mind of mine always runs around in circles, infinite.
Same landscapes and sceneries in front of these eyes.

Always talking because otherwise how will I distract myself
from the havoc that wrecks in my mind.
How do you make sense when there are wires jumbled up
with bottled things left unsaid.

When at night, time stretches beyond the hands of that wall clock,
when the monster in you whispers things that should be left unheard.
Beats of this creature inside my head,
sound like melodies drenched in poison at times,
and other times like candies made of screams and addiction.

A note strung here,
a key ripped apart there,
that most powerful music,
too much to bear.
Strangest of threads that turn into thoughts furthermore,
a string strummed with blood-stained fingers with rings of pearl amour.

Snapped gems lying on the floor,
their *pop-pop-pop* creating thunders unknown.
A gust of wind, knocking the stack of confidence that I gathered all day,
resulting in stuttering words, trying to find a way.

This is an instrument that I have yet to learn to play.
So my demons with their glasses of poison wine,
play melodies, making me the prey of my mind.
They bang their feet and start fires,
that burns bridges and leaves dire.
Memories and unwind and I am left with empty, hollow eyes

The one you don't see coming

Unknown.
Like the space between starts.
Or traces of life on Mars.
Unknown like the darkness of night or what lies behind inky skies.
Unknown like the secrets of the universe or a line from the death verse.
Unknown. Uncertain. Unpredictable.

A train that went off track,
or a bomb that blasted overhead.
A ship that was taken by the angry waves,
or perhaps a body lost, that was never found in this maze.

A plane that vanished in thin air,
and the stories that followed after care.
An accident that was never meant to take place there.

The ceiling that fell on the heads sitting on a dining table,
a building that burnt down with millions of hearts, unstable.
A live wire met with skin and tiny, small fingers.
A house that turned to ashes, resulted in closed caskets.

The death that was never solved, a mystery untold.
The theories that justified a secret that wasn't ahold.
A protest, a revolution followed by death and destruction.

Untimed death of a fellow guardian
or the rebirth of a forever lain maiden.
A laugh at night, turned to cry at dawn, oh so brazen.
A young soul lost, absolutely aghast
or the old soul that fought, for some unknown, uncertain cost.
Rise of kingdom never seen before,
fall of the one that conquered the world as a whole.

A bird's wings chopped,
and the pictures that were cropped.
A life that was poisoned,
for some crime it didn't even commit.
A miracle we call to something that's surprising in good favour
and a tragedy when it leaves in its wake, death and
destruction above all.
Something that wasn't supposed to happen after all.

But the death and destruction,
and the accident on multiple occasions,
the bus that met with the truck,
a bus of kindergartners en route to some beautiful
destination,
but tragedy struck.
And the whole lot went under the debris, crushed.

The one we don't see coming, the worst kind,
a tragedy more horrific than any crimes.
the war that broke out and we were unprepared,
no ammo, no armour and no courage,
to face something that wasn't supposed to happen.
Blood wasted, lives lost, tragedy the word on head lines,
embossed.

The most subtle surprising blows,
like change, how it's so underwhelming,
and subtle and constant and always in the making,
yet when it comes awaken,
a blow to the gut, stab in the heart, breathtaking.

Of wars and stories alike

The stories they told, of king, kingdoms and their wealth untold.
The songs they recited of marching armies and housewives frightened.
The colour they called victory, red, crimson, scarlet
With wounds and scars on their skin ivory.

Old of the house, told stories older than them.
About war, witches, battles and despair.
About how poverty struck in the midst of kingdoms divided
and living was no more than just barely surviving.

The battles that seemed endless,
with lives lost uncountable
and blood that was lost could fill entire oceans.
Of clinging swords and metal against metal.
Of broken armors and destruction, so fatal.

Waiting children, waiting maidens
for a flying word of their loved one at the front.
No words at best, words of end at worse.
Dreams of reunion, hopes of peace,
faith in king for there was no place else to put their beliefs.

From the crack of dawn to the streaks of dusk,
a battle they fought for power and blood lust.
What's the value of a mortal or two?
One or thousand it doesn't matter
when in the end power comes that banters.

These stories of war
from the time when we were unborn,
still heard and recited by scarred entities.
These stories of war that will be recited
beyond after our desolation, intensive.

Added to these stories will be
new lines and scenes to tell,
a battle unique of divided nations and mankind in despair.
A war with yourself, a war at front,
what's the difference when loss comes facing you upfront.

The wars then, and the wars now,
maybe even wars that will lead after.
The man who went to fight in ancient relics
has still not returned home after.

He will not come, and neither will we,
for this life is war, of choices and maddening thirst.
Every day you go to battlefield
in hopes of returning someday to yourself and to peace so
sweet.
Where's the end, when's the end.
What's victory and what's not.
What's winning and what will be lost.
Is it even worth it, for all that it costs.

Blurred truth and tainted dreams

Dream. I dream with my eyes open and closed,
and weave those dreams into thoughts, imagination.
I dream of the good and the bad.
I think about fireflies dancing at night,
and water with silver moon sheen.
The night owl singing it s song, oh a beautiful melancholy.

I listen to the soft breeze as it blows by
with the smell of summer so sweet.
I think garden lilies and wildflowers are free.
I imagine the most beautiful scenes.

I think about impossible futures
and sometimes impossible endings,
I think about happily ever afters,
unachievable, yet I let myself hope.

But as much as I think about flowers,
honey, water streams, musical scenes and impossible dreams,
I also dream about wars and protests,
of destruction and demons, of the world as it truly is.

I think about the blood it costs
and all the lives that were lost, will be lost.
I imagine death and graves,
coffin stones blank and un-brave.
I see a future of a thousand crushed dreams,

and I see fine little daisies stomped over by shoes and boots
and I hear rattling screams.

I see men and women, outcast,
I see someone breaking down the glass.
I see power-hungry mortals sometimes,
who crush delicate dreams and pick pieces to weave garlands,
throne and gold mines.

I see beauty and betrayal.
I see and I write.
Sometimes of love so sweet and a happy ending it meets,
other times of blood and death, and poison and malice,
of lace dipped in tar and broken toys, obsolete.

I use metaphors for the most gruesome of things,
to give it a little dress to play pretend in.
I write of hope and how it can be broken,
I write of homes and how it can be taken,
I write of love and how it can expire,
I write of lust and how it can be so dire.

I write sweet sonnets and I write ugly scenes.
Because there is always the truth,
lingering in the corner,
of how things are rather than how they should be.

So I write about what should be(s) and what-ifs and maybes,
I write about fairytales, fiction, and sweet babies.
But the truth taints everything dark and vary,
so I write about revolution and revolts, of power and position,
of death and destruction, of reality that you see through
tinted red glass,
the colour of blood and to remember how it was lost.

Healing, perhaps at last

I pick up things, from moments and more.
I put them in bottles that are over spilling since before.

I was looking for home in all the wrong places,
In people and faces,
For every wrong I wrote a write,
I apologised for the things that were never mine.

My head was singing haunted rhymes, reminding me of my every crime,
My eyes were crying hollow tears,
I wasn't wearing any surviving gear,
Submerged in my own lies,
suffocated myself with my own strangled cries.

But always taught myself to hide,
Behind words and smiles.
Let my heart sing me a song,
The lyrics repeating the same line on and on;
there is nowhere you belong.

I felt my heart break again and again,
Yet there was nowhere to hide from the pain.
I always believe that the monster was someone I just couldn't see,
But never doubted that it was all along me.

Blamed gods and beliefs,
Yet never looked enough, deep.
I was supposed to human and heart,
Alive like a spark.
But all I felt like was a sorry collection luggage left
unpacked.

Maybe(s) and what if(s), all the things that I left unsaid.
The voices that I had to drown inside my head,
Left me numb and speechless.
At times I pulled apart the skin,
To let the crimson liquid out,
The only this that made me feel and
Not some trick played by my mind and heart.

How do I unpack years of memories and moments?
How do I take this load off?
Do I put on someone else's back,
Make them love me and let them deal
With years of bottled poison and pearls.

Or do I just carry the bags and leave for some next
Destination, perplexed?
Do I spill my belongings everywhere I take shelter from
storms?
Or do I just add more and more on my back,
And take it to my grave at last?
Where I can finally heal from things that no one apologised
for,
And things that I never apologised for?
But I do wish that I would heal at last.

War Zone

I am at war with myself.
I am the bullets and the bombs.

But I'm also the one who mourns.
I was born in a world of broken
thrones and distant dreams.
Nothing could help me, for I no longer dream.

I built some bridges and then burnt each one down until;
the fire melted my flesh and gave me wounds.

I planted daisy seeds in a war field;
I watched them bloom because I
wanted to see how long vulnerable things can last.

I watched those daisies die,
covered in blood of things that no longer cry.

Daisies died and so did a part of me,
my sensitive heart turned as cold as the arctic breeze.

In that moment I made myself forget,
everything I believed and,
gave myself up to destiny and captivity.

I became a prisoner of my own mind
as I watched a part of my soul die every time .

Blamed fate for tearing me apart
but it wasn't the fate that did me wrong,
It was me, the girl who self-destructed her soul.

I laid lifeless at night hearing strangled choking,
desperate cries, though I couldn't figure out
if they were mine or of things I destroyed with a merciless mind.

Rip my heart out and I'll feel nothing.
The beats left my heart the day I started destructing.

Put bullets through my lifeless soul,
I won't feel an ounce of pain,
as the bomb ticking in my head has left me numb and
inhumane.

I've become a victim of my mind's barbaric tendencies;
my calloused self has become corrupted.

You'll see tears flowing out of my eyes like waterfalls,
but these tears no longer make sense at all.

Long gone are the days full of life,
what's left is just a war zone, with destructing fights.

I've become a battlefield;
And the fight is between me and my mind.
It's pretty clear who's going to win this fight.

My mind has the upper hand,
as I'm an emotional wreck not suitable for this war zone
where I stand.

I am in defence,
but who knew your mind could be so good in combat.

I'll destruct and so will my soul,
left will be a lifeless body with nothing to make it whole.

Blood will be everywhere,
cries will echo in the open sky,
the night will persist in all its dark glory as lightning rage
and thunderstorms
will make the dramatic scene as I'll take my last breaths,
in a war zone that's gory.

No angels will sing, no light'll shine,
and I'll die a prisoner of my own mind.

The Broken

As a child I always had a hunch for broken things,
I never threw away my broken toys, be it broken marbles,
broken pieces of plastic
I never threw away broken things,
I would always collect broken pieces of glass and other things
ruined
My mother called me the child of ruins,
For I loved anything and everything
a little battered and bruised, a little tattered and rough, a
little broken and ruined.
I always had a hunch for broken things.
I kept and collected these pieces of glass,
Like they were my most valuable treasures,
And perhaps they were.
I always had a hunch for broken things.
But as I grew up I realised this had a deeper meaning.
And maybe I am the child of ruins,
Born for darkness and rage,
And thunderstorms and mighty cages,
Maybe I was never meant for bright days and sunshine,
For I was bound to fall in love with dark and gloomy skies.
For anyone can love the mended and repaired,
I was the one made for broken things and despair,
I always had a hunch for broken things.
And I never threw away the broken pieces,
For I have a broken heart and a shattered soul.
But that doesn't mean I'll throw it away,
For I have a heart that has been broken over and over again,
But the heart though fragile, broken, vulnerable, is still mine.

I've always had a hunch for broken things.
We are all a little broken.
We are all in pieces.
For I'm not the only one who can love these ruins,
We are all children of ruins.
We were risen from the broken ashes and we will go back to the broken ashes.
I've always had a hunch for broken things.
For all can love the sweet and lovable and perfect, let me be the one to love the broken beyond repair.
Let me be known as the child of ruins,
Carve these words on the stone of my grave,
Let me be known as the warrior of dark gloomy skies,
And let these ruins merely be a speck in my dull dark mind.
I've always had a hunch for broken things.
For everyone's a little broken, and so are you mother so are you.
And let this child of yours be the reckless of all,
For being broken is in my blood, bones and soul.

Hidden Signs

Spilling off the rim, the good deeds and sins,
jars full of fireflies, hope that never dies,
sitting beside a jar of stones, green with mould.
Some over spilling some not, others just lie there forgotten,
memories and moments that got rotten.

Picking torn papers off the floor,
trying to piece them together, make them whole.
Un-aligned, tattered sides,
taped pieces with misspelt, misplaced words,
Senseless stuttering lines.
What's broken can never truly be mended.

Passed down paperbacks with broken spines,
yellowed pages, spilt wine.
Age-old pens with nips rusted from time,
streaks of ink leaking from their necks,
drawing disrupted lines.

Dried down buds and flowers in that journal, so old,
stuffed with memories that unfold,
pieces of experience stuck on pages, bold,
so filled till bounds it's hard to close.

A sweater so tattered hanging by its threads,
still safely kept in the cupboard because it's just too hard to
forget.
The very first star on your kindergarten drawing,
all stored in your mind like that first nursery rhyme.

The story books that were read at nights,
of kings and queens and princes and princesses
with love undying and all their might.
The flowers you picked and put them on your crown,
had your own coronation, became the queen of lands unbound.

Writing words and letting them stain,
your mind and memories and might, insane.
Hiding things behind a mask, drawing curtains over your wrath,
letting the flame simmer and die down,
rubbing salt on open wounds.

Putting the beast down to sleep,
with your heart and hands left to bleed.
Spilling ink on carpeted floors, hiding in corners,
all the things left unexplored.
Writing, hiding, crying and giving in and out,
doing nothing, lay about.

Letting the pen do the speaking,
this mouth closed up from not using.
Words after words making lines after lines.
Phrases, fragments, multitudes of a fearless sleepy mind.

Letting the eyes of stranger beings,
see the words that you so easily feign,
oh look about, in and out.
What's yours and what's mine,
keep your eyes closed and look around with an open mind,
read in between the lines.

You'll find love, lust and hurt in cramped spaces,
Left there to be forgotten and erased.
You'll find darkness behind all this light,
Blocked by memories alight.
You'll find pain,
In heaps and bounds.
Unhealed open founds,
And traces of blood dried down.

The Youth of Broken Thrones

Live, exist or survive,
youth of broken thrones and divided life.

Burn, burn, burn them down, burn it down,
create a wildfire, no matter what;
find a way out.

Fast or slow, in or out,
broken glasses or flowers that sprout.
Pick up the pieces, don't let them know,
don't let them see, are you bleeding, are you even breathing.
Doesn't matter if the heart's still beating.
Racing down the cliffs, fighting in mud,
dark parking lots and nights that are hot.
Rippling fear and crippling anxiety,
all hidden behind a reckless identity.

Laughs hollower than soul,
and minds darker than truths untold.
Tears from red-rimmed eyes;
A collection of grief, loss and not so good-byes.
Broken screens and broken hearts, dark minds and darker souls.

Youth of the dark, hidden behind the fog.
Dust, smoke, and rancid air,
lanky limbs attached to a body not so whole.
A friend or a foe, there's no in-between,
only enemies and people with the same enemies as you.
No unknown strangers and no soft smiles,
no knowing stories and just reciting telling your own lines.

Pill bottles and drinks unknown,
drinking elixirs, mixing potions,
all in the hopes feel alive in motion.
World revolves, dizzy hearts and revolting emotions,
all hidden behind a mask of hope.

Fighting for thrones, and then bigger thrones,
losing winning all in vain,
because it doesn't matter if you lose yourself in the midst of war.

Reality strikes like lightning bolts.
The world lived on before them and it will move on after them.
You. Me. Us.
And all our stories untold.
Souvenirs of our lives, growing mould.
It won't stop,
Not for you or me or for any mortal.
You'll live, exist or survive.
The stories of your life may or may not be told.
Either you burn bright enough to alight the worlds whole
Or you turn to ashes taking with you so much more.
But the revolution won't stop and neither will the revolt.

Tales of Men of Finery and Gold

Crisp air and gloomy lights,
dark nights,
with tales of men that destruct, reconstruct,
and bring doom to matter magic, mortals, fuel and life.

Wise women of hundred say,
be careful with your friend and foes,
choose and pick with great care,
just like the housemaid picks garden plums,
with fine eyes and delicate hands.

These women faced fires and broke ice thick,
they saw the world with clear sight,
they groomed daughters and raised fine men,
but always told, beware not all men bring home love and fair.
Rather some just bring doom and despair.

They passed on these tales of dangerous men,
their looks as deceiving as a beautiful wolf, which hides its fangs.
They always told, don't trust the captivating smiles,
a mouth that quirks up at every turn of line,
teeth so white like blinding pearls, with lips so plump,
like rose and honey dripping candy plums.

Don't trust their high and mighty chests,
and their lean strong legs,
with palms so smooth and alluring and fingertips so soft,
make you want to give your heart in their hands.
They do with it what they please,
and do it so beautifully that you won't even care.

They cage you in their gold chains
and wrap you in fine silks,
they choke you with strings made of flowers
and collar your neck with diamonds and stones,
and they do it all so assuringly,
that you so willingly follow them home.

They make you a prisoner of their smiles and easy way,
they make you laugh and then they make you cry,
they feed on your blood, they make you lust,
you show them love and they show you cruelty,
they laugh at your miseries and you smile in their chains.
You feel peculiarly beautiful, playing their games.

Don't trust these men,
they are more dangerous than any filthy monster looking
creature,
for they come dressed in fine silks, and embroidered gold.
They look nothing like the monster they hide within
themselves,
they look like princes and make you feel like a damsel in distress.

Don't trust these men,
for they see the world as it could be,
bring about what they want rather than what it should be.

Absences Beyond

Decorating empty spaces.
How can one ever find an escape to these mazes?

For every loss, there is a flower planted in my gardens,
and a memorandum written in my heart.
For every space, that was once filled but now remains empty,
is decorated with crystal,
vines and music plays in the background, sublime.

I've hung tapestry to cover these empty voids,
holes devoid of life.
I've hung lanterns, that my tears fuel,
on both sides of darkness whole.
Illuminating the entrance, but showing nothing beyond.
I like it like that, decorated and dusted,
so that it doesn't feel as empty.

I sing apologies in my head, ***I'm sorry-I'm sorry.***
I tune these beg-pardons to the sound,
to the melody of my cries.
I play music, if sad rhymes so that
the lingering hand of doom can sway left and right.

Some absences I plaster,
only for the concrete to chip away.
And with a gust of wind when the tapestry falls,
exposing these empty kins.
I silently grieve for what was once within.
Then I pin up more covers,
to hide the space, the nothingness.

And I dig some mud up to bury more.
I dig graves, and I put memory stones,
For things that were never known.
And pluck my flowers of loss,
and leave them in the mud to die alone.
Then I sing songs of legend and wars.
I birth my poetry in death, loss and beyond.

I prepare feasts, for what's yet to come.
I feed it with my hands, and I let it rest,
I look after it, do my best.
And then I dug up mud some more,
with the same hands that pulled blankets over sleeping forms,
and made sweets and candies and fed them whole.

I lay down, another absence, I lay down some more.
Then I plant the flower of loss and let it bloom,
only for it to be plucked, and left to gloom.

Then I start over again,
to welcome warmth only for it to leave me devoid and drought.
Then I let it go,
and conduct more funerals and make more burials.
I decorate the absence with flowers and poems.

Leave, stay

Come in, my doors are always open.
Come, you're welcome here.
Just be careful, I'm fragile.
I come in a box that's labelled with red bold letters "caution".

Be cautious, don't touch anything,
and don't move about too fast,
you'll collide with a stack of bravery I collected all my life.
Don't try to fix it, don't try to break it.
Leave it be.
Leave me be.

Don't try to clean the mess on the carpet.
My clothes scattered along with my emotions.
Don't rummage through drawers,
you'll find broken promises and
my collection of unrealistic classics.

Don't leave your fingerprints.
Don't leave your footprints.
I have enough scars to last me a lifetime and if not more.
Don't try to break down my walls,
once they break the water they've been holding in will flood out
and I won't be able to clean out my own mess.
The paint has already started peeling and the cracks aren't
even healing.

Leave.

I won't stop you.
I can't force you to stay.
Doors are open, they are always open.
Entry, exit

Just don't take anything with you.
Don't leave your remnants behind,
without your memories and mementoes,
It'll be slightly easier to erase you
with my tears and the cloth of stolen moments.

Don't leave reciting my favourite lines,
don't go telling me that fault is not mine.
I'm still holding onto the past,
and the people that did me wrong.

I'm bleeding,
And suffocating, barely breathing,
The memories are choking.
Healing has stopped,
I'm waiting for breathing to do the same.
This lie or life is horridly mundane.

Why'd you mark my walls with your frames,
it was my heart and not your living space.
You left the door open,
And now the rain if staining my doorway,
And the mud is seeping in.

You came, and you left.
I wish it was that easy for me.
But here I am, with a bucket full of sins,
And a rag with ink stains,
trying to wipe down your existence and your prints.

Ruination

Collateral damage, I bought.
Everything I touched either decayed or turned to dust.

Hurting, came to me easy.
Hurting, myself or others,
It was like my reflex for every quarry,
Every rubble.

Everyone I ever loved,
Was left drained and unloved.
Addicted or close to combusting.
Looking for answers in my destructing.

I break myself to pieces,
And then take the sharp ones,
And mark things I love.
A proof of the monster in me,
That chains things and never lets them go unscathed or free.

I destroy things along with the remnants of me.
And then I cry for their loss,
And make them memories.
I let them fade, like the scars on my hands and waist.
But never truly let them go,
Because I'm selfish and hunt more and more.

I whine for my crimes, but never once stop.
These sins are always a reminder of what I destroyed
And what I lost.
Once you've become so monstrous,
How do you ever stop?

I drench myself in love, kindness and dreams.
I become exactly what people need.
But then I smell vulnerability,
And I prowl and hiss,
Attacking so slow that it's no less than pure bliss.

I pick some flowers from the blooms of those,
Whom I damaged and ruined so up close.
And then I use those fragrant little beings,
To decorate myself for a different story, different scene.

I brew sweet poisons in my free time,
And drip my desserts in that toxic fine.
But remember this that I never once stop crying.
The devil in me, feeds on love, and vulnerability and fear,
First mine and then others.

I keep fueling my demons,
They don't let themselves starve,
And I am merely their slave,
Thoroughly chained, doing whatever they say.

I am the epitome of ruination,
Every flower I touch dies,
Every bird I adore loses flight,
Every person I love dies inside.
And after every conquest I am left with more pieces,
And more funerals to abide.

At last, I've become a graveyard of my own.
With mud still damp, from the last rain and last storm.
The flowers on the last grave haven't even wilted yet,
And here I am making more space,
burying more love, birthing more hate.

Paint and Hide

Take out my canvas and try to paint life,
but all that comes to mind,
is blank spaces with empty faces,
and no signs of smiles.

Open drawers and paint bottles,
hard brushes and tender touches.
Hard strokes, soft smokes.
Drop, drop, drop, colour here and colour there,
a cacophony of beautiful destructing things,
all and stories, unfair.

Singing lines and reciting vines,
melancholy skies and lost and hazy eyes.
Songs of pain, and cries of night,
mixed together in something so much more than
what could be just might.

Yellows, and blues and whites, colours of life,
with emotions hidden behind every drip and tide.
Horizons of end, sunsets of war lights,
morning of beginnings and nights of cries.
Whining rain drops, scary storms, melting snow
And un- healing wounds.

Scars given by life,
battles that were mandatory to fight,
a war you didn't sign up for,
love that only gave way to betrayal,
pain that didn't make you any stronger,
pieces that were broken and lost.

Mistakes and taints and memories unwanted.
Taunts, labels and boxes of sizes,
decided by outsiders and ancestors, unregarded.

A drop wrong, a stroke out of place,
permanent marks with nothing to hide the pain.
Try and try with the white so light,
to hide the dark that came uninvited.

Coat after coat, gallop after gallop to cover the black,
to hide it behind layers of light.
Cover, cover, cover no one should see what
lies behind sparkly smiles and red-rimmed eyes.

Try and try, in hopes to leave it behind,
the black and the dark that no one wants in light.
No matter what you do it always shows through,
cracked layers and uneven paint coats ,
so everyday you apply a new layer,
to the things you want to hide.
Yet at the end of the day,
they always come back to haunt you at night.

But isn't that just life,
you cry and you hide,
you laugh and die on the inside,
you break and glue the pieces back together,
you put your faith in things unchained, only for it to be broken.
you're given hope only for it to be shattered,

How many times have you been given hope when none
should be given at all?
And in the end do you reminisce about everything you ever lost?

Of Poetry and Death

Inevitable, it's called, for a reason after all.
Inescapable, tying, bound to come, to fall.
For being inescapable we have made it a conquest,
to make the end memorable in all our vest.

For what's the glorious of all,
to die fighting or perhaps giving up after struggling for too long.
Maybe naturally. maybe not.
Untimed, ill-timed, perhaps not knowing when to fall.

Given a choice to pick your downfall,
would you choose battle scars or soft silks
or maybe earthy mud and rough ground,
or twinkling stars above all.

Wrapped up in white sheets or a flag of some sort,
coffin or fire, maybe rotting after all.
An accident untimed, when the clock strikes nine,
poison of various kinds.

Mystery, melancholy, murder, might.
Sweet memories, good stories,
whatever you did was bright.

If it were up to me I'd choose simplest of all
or perhaps simple for me and grand for all.
I'll meet my end wearing a white dress,
covered in my life stories and conquests.
Surrounded by poems while processing poetry,
in the midst of the most beautiful cacophony.

With my last breaths of life,
will leave metaphors gloomy and bright.
With my arms covered in ink
and my hands dripping with bloody sins.

Parchment, papers, scrapes.
Pieces, patience all snapping apart.
I'll let my life crumble like a day old crust.
Surrounded by books with broken spines,
worn with time, like my body and soul untwine.

The light'll leave my eyes,
as I'll imagine a scene of fireflies and beautiful lies,
pockets full of buttons and pins,
a scene of love as equally good as unholy sins.

Coffee stains and spilt drink,
a night too long met by a morning too short.
Stopping words and slowing beats.
A sudden end, a full stop to all things bottled in me.

If it were up to me, I'll welcome death with open arms,
I'll meet it as a friend
Meeting finally after these long roads end.
I'll let out a hearty laugh,
tell it that all my life I used it as a metaphor.
I am writing words right now and I will leave thinking about more,
but all I can do beyond is perhaps risk some hope.

PART TWO

Of The Blood,
And The Bones.

Musicale

It doesn't matter what you think.
What if it's an act, this body and all the strings attached?
Paper-thin skin, with veins within, what if it's all a sin?

I've written countless lines,
un-punctuated, in that diary of mine
with yellowed pages.
I've held close my kindness
with my sins sitting side by side.
I've looked upon the mistakes,
and have cried a thousand times;
yet committed more and more crimes.

Dance, that's what this life feels like,
a musicale that has me reciting practised lines.
Every day a new act is played,
But what if I'm not prepared for today?
But you don't get a choice,
it's a luxury I can't afford.
For what it costs, I'm broke,
my shame and guilt will eat me alive,
and that's a price I'm not willing to abide.

Wear those shoes, point those toes,
don't stumble, just cope.
Skid across the floor with grace,
don't care if your mind is running an endless race.
Stutter and they'll know, fall and it'll show.
What goes down in your mind are you really willing to show?

Are you tired? Run on intoxicated brews,
but perform even though you don't want to.
Those blisters on your feet, do they *hurt?*
But if you don't act, this mind will drench your soul, straight and curt.
Learn the rhythm and the lines,
go off beat and your cries will be heard throughout the night.

Sin, sin some more,
you have to survive, so commit some more.
Write your script, from the world's point of you,
After all, no one cares what's true.

Smile, plaster it, paint it, if you must.
Nobody likes it when those lips are down turned.
Drip them in cherry, glaze it with honey,
make sure your words are sweeter than candy.

Lust if you must, give them a show.
So what if you're falling apart, none should know.
Get on your knees, do some splits,
strain harder, don't resist.

Cry, no one's stopping you,
but do it in the dark of night,
and by the morning, these rules you shall abide.
Staring at the exit door won't grant you freedom sweet,
you're your own captive, someone you're not willing to free.

Fit in, with the crew, oh you're a solo act,
then smile through and through.
Pick up your belongings when the show is done,
but come back tomorrow and do this over and over.

When the sun hits your window in the morning,
wipe your ink-stained hands on your rags,
close that diary, you have to *act.*

Home not Art, my shelter picked apart

Picked apart. Pulled together.
What was once home is an ornament now and safe no more.

Scrub, flip, don't let the paint chip.
Paint, hide, make it pristine.
Polish, burnish, make it shine.
Gloss, wax, grease those rough lines.

Picking, pulling, ripping apart,
with eyes glossy like glass.

Colour that skin, make it bright.
Whatever you are hiding behind that crooked smile.
Align those stars in your eyes so vast,
it's supposed to be art.
Make it appealing. Make it prim.
Have no boundaries, blur those sins.

Line those eyes, look humble and wise.
Hammer those bones, that jut out whole.
Colour those lips, plump and crisp.
With cheeks flushed, no matter if from thirst.
Sandpaper those edges, smooth those scars,
and if you cannot, hide them behind masks.

* * *

Drip, drip, drip. Last of what's left drips.
Snap, snap, snap. The last thread finally snaps.
Skin tears, eyes water, blood boils hotter.
Home, it's called, inescapable of all.
Your own skin that you behold.

Painted white, changed was the colour of warm light.
Because dusk is only alluring when it's a scenic sight.
And red's only cherry when your lips are dripping
and your cheeks are flushed, right.

So this home became impersonal more and more.
Decorations were added that had no sentiment at all.
Lanterns were hung; brighter than the sun,
the fuel to light them was my peace, overrun.

The fire that cackled was to keep warm,
Not burn the whole abode to ground.
The music was to keep company
and not to drown the horrendous cacophony.
The walls were painted with the colour of my existence
but peeled apart to varnish and shine,
keep it persistent.

The furniture was a collection of memories,
of spilt wine and ink fine and poetry unwind.
The carpet was scarle t, just like my blood,
It gave me hope and horror all at once.
But the floors were ripped, and couches thrown,
to make space for things that I barely owned.

Stranger things, filled my bones;
How am I even supposed to call it home?
Cries were heard louder than chatter,
that filled these rooms, uninvited, untethered.
Guests arrived late at night, to have a drink, and show their might.
They looked around and danced gloom,
their breathing- a peculiar sound, stunted all my blooms.

They said it's art, to ponder and stare.
They said it's unholy and bare.
They said it's raw and altered it un-fair.
They said it's supposed to be seen and shared.

What was supposed to be a sanctuary
is no more than a museum display now.
To be looked at, but not to be held.
To be stared at, but never to be cherished.
To be gazed upon because it is strange.
To be wondered about, to be laid bare.
What was home once, is a prison now.
How can one even find a way out?

Mirror, please lie to me

Mirrors don't lie now, do they?
They show you exactly the things,
you whispered never to see, when you prayed.

The reflection that shines,
The image you'd like to erase from your mind.
Hating the way the reflection mocks you every time.

Making no eye contact with yourself,
Because you're so terribly ashamed.
And how every time you look, you spot some new flaws
In every corner, every nook.

When the mirror that was to look and admire,
Became your worst enemy and burned all desire.
When you no longer laughed,
With your eyes crinkled and cheeks flushed.

Should've shattered that looking glass in half,
When it started deciding your self worth at last.
But it isn't that easy, right,
Because we've been made to look for validation in every
crevice that will suffice.

We were put in boxes from the moment we were born,
These boxes labelled with different songs,
But never to be tampered with.
These boxes, no matter if too small,
Let them suffocate you and your soul.

So you beg and cry and bleed,
You go down on your knees,
And you let the tears and blood stain your body and cheeks.
You keep screaming- ***show me the things that i want to see,***
mirror-mirror please lie to me.

- Beauty that destroys and the mirror used
  as a weapon in disguise.

Galaxies Inside

The big bang happened, for some unknown reason,
the stars collided and the atoms were guided,
to a path where the beings were livable and lovable united.

Our body's a composition of elements
and materials that are traced back to
being 14 billion years old, we are the universe we see,
it that way, we are the stars that we long.

We were and are the part of something big,
and it's a part of us,
so what's valid and what's not who are we to decide
when we can't even suffice the galaxies in us.

The other day I picked up a book that read
about the beauties of love and lust,
I kept it down and thought,
how significant the stars would be if
they were thrown at our feet,
and how the sky would've been magnificent
if it was just in our reach.

We preach the stars and the universe unknown,
we think of it as mysterious, and hollow yet so full of everything,
we think of the distance between stars
and how we cross it,
we think of all the things that we just couldn't have.

Looking at my palms, the lines of a jagged space,
how would I love this universe
if I could place it on my hand and toy with its face.
So I drew some blood and stained my hands,
thinking I tainted the magnificent beast,
with the blood of a mortal that weeps.

I thought of world, parallel and more,
and entrances to whole new souls.
I thought of black holes and white ones too,
and I thought of asteroids that derange whole spheres alone.
I thought of the cosmos and what lies within,
the nebulas and it's unknown definition.

I tried wondering what escapes the dark holds,
does it get you places or eat you whole.
Will colours that look so bright, burn my skin stark and white.
Will the edges of a rough flight tear my skin
and make it a bloody limp less pile.

Or perhaps there is more to see,
to discover and to heal.
There are provinces beyond sight,
perhaps a ruler in all its glory and might,
or maybe we are just the toys,
in the hands of that potency's plight.
Are we merely just the puppets in this game
we thought of we purely rule.

I was looking around,
going round and round,
what I didn't realise was that what I was looking desperately for
was residing in myself and in my wounds.
That all this time I was bleeding the cosmos profound.

So one last time I slit open my wrists
and let the crimson stain my body and face and my lips,
I drank the universe, and let the stars float,
these scars on my body no less than constellations rewrote.

The veins, strange and dismantled,
like stars unaligned, possibilities and futures up for a gamble.
Life at stake, lust and desire always win,
closing in, over taking.

Under the bed with heavy blankets,
bitten cuticles and half nails,
wreaking havoc in mind,
heart drenched inside suffocating confines.

Clawing at skin, that contained galaxies within,
the sorrowful eyes crying tears of might,
the nebula inside your head,
capable of all the good and all the bad.
The limbs attached that feel like led.

From day to night,
all I did was think of escapes divine,
but how does one escape
when whole universes reside within their soul,
inside a body where stardust and asteroids
and black holes were a hold.

I was wondering about spaces unknown,
when all I had to do was close my eyes and look inside,
I am made of the universe,
and the universe is made of me,
I need it like it needs me.
I am made of galaxies and constellations beyond,
I am made of skin and bone and sun and planets prolong.

I am a miracle,
and so is every one that walked this place,
so when you're bleeding all over again,
realise that you're letting worlds and universes go to waste.

Self

This is an ode to your fearless self.
For your beautiful you.

For the times you've apologised for being too loud,
or simply just expressing yourself the way you ought.

For the times you've painted yourself neutral beige,
because your lovely vivid colours appeared too staged.

For the times you felt sorry for your skin, size or might,
for the times when you totally gave up the fight.

For the times you constructed bridges
and burned them down for the sake boundaries,
love and pressure from all around.

For the times you wished to be quiet and slow,
and hidden in background curtains,
when it was your own damn show.

For the times you had to tame your wild,
because apparently the world wasn't ready
for your brave and fierce soul so fine.

For the times you've tried so hard to blend,
when all your strong, strange, bright,
and beautiful wanted to shine.

For the time you apologised for taking space,
existing and being here or being there,
for all times you've been sorry,
when all you should have been was glowing with fire alight..

Stop apologising, for things that make you and add to you,
stop saying sorry and feeling sorry,
you're meant to be vivid and unique and outstanding,
you're meant to be yourself unapologetically.
You're here now; you exist, so might as well just live.

Younger Self

I remember you, my younger self,
sitting on the ground and catching ants,
I remember you with chocolate-covered hands
and candies stuffed in your mouth,
I remember you.
Come back, please.

You dancing in the rain,
you dancing on table,
with or without music it doesn't matter.
Come back, I don't dance anymore.

You waking up early on summer mornings,
running out to the garden at the crack of dawn,
getting mud on your PJs and grinning with all your teeth out.
Come back, I feel endlessly sleepy now.

You with both your cheeks stuffed with sugary cookies,
getting sugar on your clothes, sneaking cookie dough,
while mother is heating the oven,
you sitting on the counter
with your legs dangling and your face stuffed.
Come back, I don't eat anymore.

You coming back from school,
mother waiting for you at the door,
you run up and hug her,
she smells like cinnamon and her perfume,
like rose and vanilla and butter and sunlight and breeze and home.
Come back, I don't hug mother anymore.

You, when being sent to your room
was the biggest punishment ever,
being grounded was the worst thing that could ever happen.
Come back I don't go out anymore,
come back I don't come out of my room anymore.

To the little girl, in a pink tutu and fairy wings,
with a crown atop her messy hair.
Barefoot running around chasing dragonflies,
come back I miss you.

You at the town's annual fair,
Your eyes twinkling more than any fairy lights,
The list of things that you want and the rides you want to try,
All prepared in your bright mind.
Come back, my mind is not bright anymore.

Christmas lists, and birthdays presents,
Whatever you want already prepared,
Toys, games, dresses and bikes,
You've always been different, my child.
Come back, I've stopped wanting things anymore.

You lighting up the room, charming everyone,
You being loved, you existing beautifully,
You living your life to the fullest.
Come back, I'm not loved anymore.
Come back, I'm merely existing.
Come back, I've forgotten how to breathe.

Come back, I lost you.
Come back, I loved you but I don't love myself anymore.
Come back, I don't belong to myself anymore.
Come back, I'm not whole anymore.
Come back, I've lost the way.
Come back, I believe in you but not myself.
Come back, this world is scary
and you were the bravest, boldest person I ever knew.
Come
back, please.

I Met a Woman Once

I met a woman once, ordinary,
nothing special about her except
when she opened her mouth to speak,
her words sharp like razor, unfiltered, at times unholy,
ragged and cold made you cling to her
like you were a half and she was a whole.

I met a woman once,
a creation made by gods and angels
and monsters and Satan.
Soft and hard, mild and wild.
She told me that she was evil
and then laughed out loud, high and sharp.

She told me she was mad and made friends in the dark.
And yet she was the one who held me
and told me that I was art.

I met a woman once,
who was colder than ice and made of vice,
yet she loved like dainty lace
and coloured daisies and birds of paradise.

I met a woman once,
who had lived for a thousand years if not more,
she told me I was fierce in ways no one could summon.

I met a woman once,
bright like the light of a thousand fires,
she made her embers my pillow
and her flames my blanket and lulled me to sleep,
when the creatures of the dark,
The demons came hunting for meat.

She made me drink her magic
and quietened the voices in my head,
she made me hers, in more ways than I could name.

I met a woman once and then she died,
her last words were "my child you're art and sometimes
your value is realised when you're no longer here
and there or anywhere in reach."
She said "my child you're, but not something to be stared at
or picked apart.
You hold so much power that these mere mortals can't even
think about ."

I met a woman once,
wise and kind and as old as the folk rhymes,
I saw her breathing,
I saw her laughing,
I saw her dancing with the creatures of the dark
and then I saw how death does each one of us apart.

What's Holding You (Me) Back?

What's holding you back?
Your mind, your soul or your beliefs.

What's holding you back?
The love, the hate or the promises you ought to keep.

What's holding you back?
The fear or the malice.

What's holding you back?
It is the dark or the light, perhaps the day or the night.

What's holding you back?
your prayers or the lack thereof.

What's holding you back?
Your gods or your devils.

What's holding you back?
The spoken or the unspoken, is it the silence or chaos,
perhaps the quiet or the crowd.

What's holding you back?
The ignorance or arrogance?

What's holding you back?
The regret or the guilt.

What's holding you back?
Mistakes or sitting still.

What's holding you back my love?
You yourself or the things you're bound to.
Do you fear the dark or does the light blind you?

What's holding me back, perhaps my words or my fears.
Is it the insecurity or my tears?

What's holding me back?
Doubts that sprout or actions that I ought.

What's holding me back?
Perhaps the ink and the pages.

What's holding me back?
The confidence or the lack thereof.

What's holding me back?
Giving up or the battle recklessly fought.

What's holding me back?
What's holding you back?

You are chained and so am I.
We are chained, these knots we can't untie.
Close your eyes, look deep inside,
What's holding you back?

Take a look in your mind perhaps it would unravel,
Secrets, dreams and memories scattered.

What's holding you back?
Beliefs, promises, or perhaps the world,
Travelled-untraveled.

What Lies Within

What are you hiding?
What are you blaming?
What are your illusions?
What are you pretending?

Skilled liars is what we are,
because after all you don't just show your true colours,
To be fed on and ripped apart.

What illusions are you keeping?
Are they about love, lust or something more ?

Are you blinded by your gods
or do you worship the devil now ?

Do you still think about the past
or is the future all you want now ?

What are you pretending?
Trying to be blind when the light is all that shines.
Don't you really see the truth or are you nose deep in ignorance.
Is it you that's winning or the arrogance ?

What are you hiding?
Your desires or your lies.
Are you putting up the show for us to see,
and you to live in,
while in the dark of the night you let your true self whine.

What are your secrets?
Are they too soft or too hard,
are they undesirable or desire is all you want,
What are your secrets?
Is it the money you hold so dearly, or
your screams that you hide when a nightmare strikes.

What are the lies that you tell and the lies that you have been
told?
What are the lies that make you so bold?
Are you thriving and striving for something more
or is this life of pretending all you know?

You are a liar. And so am I.
There are some things you better keep.
Because after all blood is just tainted water if you don't see.

Invisibility

Invisibility came to me as home,
A comfort that shouldn't be comfort at all.

Tired of being unloved, as I thought I was,
I mastered the art of being invisible.
That even my breath couldn't be heard in the cold.
Made as little noise as one could.
That I became a tale, a folklore of my own.

Stopped speaking, started writing,
Thoroughly forgot to look for silver linings.
Flinched in crowds, cowered under baggy clothes I ought.
I prisoned myself, sentenced a life in cell,
For what crimes, that existed and was meant live,
Not to survive.

Invisibility came as a heavy cloak,
Put over my shoulders, I could barely hold.
real - unreal slipped from mind,
I felt like an abstract, to sit still and then die.
I felt real only when I was being touched,
And when I could see my blood.

So blood became my anchor,
And torn, split skin, my home.
During day I was a shadow, barely there,
Lurking in corners, making no movement here and there.
But by night, the shadows came to life,
And no longer hidden by screams and tears and cries,
Finally came alight.

Falling in love with the wrong things

How can I not love my own filth,
When it gives me worlds and words on stilts.

I am falling in love with all the wrong things,
The damage and destruction,
The bloodshed and the violence.
I am adoring all the wrongs, writing poetries,
Turning them into metaphors.

I am falling in love with the wrong things,
The anger and the hate.
The ruins and renders.
I am making dark my muse,
And letting the light fade.

I am falling in love with the wrong things,
Make this home a prison cell,
And the romanticising captivity and hell.
I am letting my words love the filth and the guilt,
I am letting them run, reconstruct, destroy, rebuild.

I am falling in love with the wrong things,
The broken temples and torn beliefs,
Been reading stories of gods
Yet being attracted to devil sweet.

I am falling in love with the wrong things,
Because I've turned myself into a wrong being.
Where once light shined, now only darkness resides,
Broke so much, of myself and of life.

I am falling in love with the wrong things,
With pain and its idea,
With panicking when every time
Someone asks me "how are you ?"

I am falling in love with the wrong things,
With emptiness and how I'm always alone.
And if not I make sure im left be,
Normalising this captivity.

I am falling in love with the wrong things,
With crying and whining,
And how every gust of wind knocks me silent.
I am decorating this space with gory frames,
And letting black ink and poison stain this maze.

I am falling in love with the wrong things,
With harming and breaking and committing sins.
With closing curtains and locking doors,
Every time someone tries to come in.

I am falling in love with the wrong things,
With shadows and lurking monsters,
That I use in my poems.
The voice inside my head, that whispers
Awful terrible things and screams when i try to
Drown it out.

I am falling in love with the wrong things,
Like the monster in me that gnaws at life,
The devil that says no goodbyes,
The demons that fight the light,
And the funerals that I conduct all the time.

Strings

A flash before the eyes, a demon in disguise.
A word of misery and despair
or perhaps happiness so beautiful, it's utterly unfair.
A string of moments, chained scenes,
sequenced - unsequenced, a provoking flare.

As fine as strands of hair
or a silk thread woven as delicate as morning air.
A drop adding to the ocean
in a far place somewhere,
a line parallel, never ending or meeting,
running side by side till ends meet their ends.

A seed sown, fruits it might bear,
completely unknown, consequences so prone.
A garland needled through
with flowers from every garden of our minds.
Processed like age-old wine.

A thread turned fabric turned garment,
a small existence of mere solitude
turned reality enchanting.
Bead after bead, an endless chain,
binding or freeing all in your head.

Thinking- over- under. Not at all.
Numb, null and void, taking a fall.
How a fine strand in your mind
turns to a million thoughts,
how it becomes a string with multiple slots.

Sins

When hate subsided, it gave way anger,
Another one of the seven sins.
Wrath so hot that it seared all my skin and bones,
And it burned my home.

Fire filled my eyes, and left me blazing and alight,
I was angry at the world, *I still am, but I handle it better now.*
I was angry and people, places and all these empty faces.
So mad that I didn't mind turning my own self to ash,
And burning bridges at last.

I seared my own skin,
because of the blood that was burning within.
Didn't see who or didn't see why,
Just channelled this wrath in whatever that complied,
And in the end I was the one who had to gather the ashes
and cry.

Anger is a demanding emotion.
It gives you heat that burns our insides and the outsides,
And by the time it fades there is nothing left to subside.
When I was done burning homes and abodes,
All that was left was exhaustion and remorse.

The vexation faded so did the burn marks,
But not completely,
always reminding me why it's called a sin after all.
Wrath left me exhausted, it burned my motive and my plight,
I was surprisingly left hollow when it said its goodbyes.

When wrath died, it bought envy in light,
Another sin, another story, another way I ruined my life.
It consumed so whole, that I forgot how to be kind and whole.
Envy, eats your heart and then your mind,
It leaves utter darkness behind.

I looked at people, and I couldn't see past their
Happiness, wealth or might.
I didn't see faces, I saw all that they had and I didn't,
I wished bad upon them,
So that their smiles could fade,
And I wouldn't have to be happy for them and lie.

I let envy, contaminate me like poison ivy,
A jealousy so strong, made gnaw good things whole.
Perfect bodies, perfect faces, why are they smiling,
Can't they see that I'm breaking inside?
The world keeps revolving, and the time keeps ticking,
It doesn't stop for one, it doesn't stop for two.
Resentment, growls and it prowls,
It makes you the wolf you do not ought.
It looks for prey, to attack and lay,
It chews on kindness and throws it out,
It fills you with so many self-doubts.

The green-eyed monster, after destroying,
Also demised, its departure left me breading and dying.
So hollow, so dark, it covered everything
In dark vines.
Its departure bought this unfamiliar unknown rhyme,
How could I face the light again after living in confines?

Envy departed.
But a new guest arrived,
Lust and greed in all their might.
These two wreaked the most havoc of all,
Subtle but consuming all.

The lust I got, wasn't for being touched at all,
I lusted for happiness and escape,
To free myself from this fate.
And I lusted for kindness,
In my words and actions and in others same.

A little honey to bring me home,
To keep me warm, when my bones are
Rattled by thunder.

I lusted for touch, but gentle and soft,
To be held and to be taught.
And for desire so deep,
That it made even the angels weep.

But when lust is not fulfilled, it turns to greed.

And the desperation and desire brought home greed.
For the same reasons lust has walked on feet .
I played pretend, with myself and my lands,
To be loved and to be freed.

A greed so deep, it made me play roles,
Of house maidens sweet,
Who pluck plums from trees,
And bake bread and keep clean.

When blood turns tar, and heart turns concrete,
All you look for is sweet eyes and a mouth that breathes.
And you crave gentle things desperately,
And when you try to speak only soft clouds
Come free.

When lust left and greed demised,
I was finally free,
But being confined to things for too long,
Had made me forget what it felt to be free.
What do I do when I am no longer in captivity?

Letting go

The last of what's left,
I'm letting go of the darkness and the toxins,
I'm done hating, myself and the world,
I'm done surviving, I'm done existing,
So let's live and learn and let go,
Let's start this road of acceptance and hope,
You and I hand in hand,
We will let hope in again.

- Let's hope again, let's risk it,
The most lethal of things let's face it.

PART THREE

Finally Opening The Blinds, Letting The Light Shine

Lasting, Un-lasting

Turning the pages of an old journal,
Line after line scribbled, splotches of ink,
droplets faded and absorbed.
An old file on the laptop,
cursor blinking after the last word,
as if waiting to be continued.

A full stop marking the end, but the extract is yet to go on.
Paragraphs, looking finished and complete,
Feigning an end, but the cursor still blinks,
as if pleading for more, perhaps a word or an epic or folklore.

Sometimes I read my old poems, and pros, I
read and read and feel nothing of that sorts.
These long written words;
nothing more than a museum, an old historical fort.
To be admired and it's relics to be read,
don't move or change or its whole being will collapse.
You understand or you don't,
you just stare and try to figure out
What is the purpose of this all?

I stare at these phrases, I wrote them too.
Yet I can't wrap my head around these things
on paper and screen I poured.
Am I the same person as before?
Back then, was I different being all the more?

I read and read and re-read again,
words of sorrow, despair and pain.
Grief and brutality all I've known.
I feel gratitude and envy
and something mysteriously unknown.

I realise that I changed for better or worse,
that's for time to tell, the grief faded at the back of my head,
the pain drowned and riptides smoothed,
the ocean, reckless and once dangerous became tranquil and calm.
I write still, about death and dreams, and brutality and beauty,
I write still about destruction and war,
but there's this sense of calm that wasn't there before.

I turn the pages and scroll some more,
my eyes come in contact with cries of help, pain untold.
I can sense the panic in-between the lines,
I can feel how much those two hands shook
while writing these words forgotten with time.
I see scratches and scribbles, I
see chaos and calm at war, I see more of who I was.

I see demons lurking at the corner of pages,
I see the monster, hanging on door hinges,
and I see remnants of belief shattered and torn,
I see gods and demons on each shoulder, adorned .

So I slam the book shut and smack the screen close,
I realise that change wasn't so brutal after all.
It was perhaps needed and required,
that happiness is something you don't just acquire.

I see the person I was and the person I am,
one with eyes and the other in words.
I seek help and meaning and happiness and light.

I closed my fists tight and did not give up the fight.
I wrote a long time ago that hope is lethal and gore,
but so was this very same galaxy before we were born.

This hope might be dangerous and fragile,
it shatters with so much as a gust of wind slightly out of time,
but perhaps if the whole galaxy devours on it and feeds itself,
why can't us humans break and fix ourselves again ?

So I did the only thing I promised not to,
I recollected my hope and left it everywhere I wanted to.
It broke in a nook and grew in another cranny,
it's nature to break beyond repair
yet return every time stronger than thunderous air.

I broke down and then I broke down some more,
I cried and whined yet held my fists tight.
And here I am today writing this poem,
in what I think is my version of faith and hope.
This my ode to anyone who thinks
change won't bring spring after cold winter has been borne,
this is my song, and i desperately plead you sing it,
when the demons are lurking and making their ways,
Sometimes you just have to wing it.

I hope you realise that you'll change
and so will times and phases.
That you'll leave behind so much love even in your worst traces.
But at the end of the day, prepare yourself that nothing lasts,
nor war neither destruction,
even if spring comes and stays for a long time,
realise that this hope and happiness will too fall apart.
But it'll grow again in unexpected spaces,
It will only fall to get up again,
It will die only to rise from its grave.

Running and arriving

Picked up a pen, to stain some pages,
write some words, a million or ten.
I could feel from the brims of my heart,
to the tips of my finger, blood, ink,
pain to taint me and my efforts vain.

Overfilling, spilling around the edges,
these words, broken promises and empty pledges.
So I braced my hands and heart and paper,
to face the might of a thousand senators.
Yet not once the field was stained, the attack never even came.

Tried again to let out these suffocaters,
too stubborn to listen to, these heartless traitors.
Closed my lids, heavy as lead,
with too much care and too much to bear,
the hurricane inside, a never-ending despair.

Learnt so far, from battles and scars,
that art can't be forced and runs a million miles per hour.
Sometimes towards you other times away;
you never know its destination until it's as close as flesh,
and skin and bones, or like stars and galaxies
and constellations, further away.

It runs right off its hinges, for better or worse,
you have to wing it, it's a blessing and a curse.
It suffocates and chokes at times,
and is free to move whenever it feels fine.

Your words rattle and cry yet don't flow when you try.
These words put themselves in coffins and caskets,
burn to ashes inside these spaces.
Rebirthed from the shadows, from corners darker than ink
and night.
Splatter and spill and smudge and dye,
your beats, your soul and your mind.

Realising this and so much more,
sometimes your art runs away from you
only to find its way back home.
Chaos and calm, two of its traits,
constantly present in its absence and in its wake.

The candle of your soul,
snuffed out, only to light back brighter than before.
The flames die down only to rise again as a Phoenix with its
fiery wings.
It's feather alight, like the sun so bright,
it's eyes spark and beak so sharp,
symbol of might and a new start.

Stuck on pages, imagination and drought,
dying lilies, rotten gardens and weeds that sprout.
Pluck and pull and claw and scrub.
Pick and snatch and smash and cry,
let that hope inside of you die.
Gnaw and bite and pinch and snide, the flesh on your body,
Give up the fight?

Time's a weapon, lethal and more.
It's no one's but itself as whole,
it takes and leaves and gives and reduces.
It teaches and preaches and stops for none,
it can heal and also destroy one.

So you wait patiently, though you don't want to,
what's yours will come back to you at dusk or dawn.
It's in the roots, just hidden behind,
Curtained under some fog and mist and blackness blind.
The clouds clear one day or another,
what was pulled further, gravitates back home bringing love
and laughter,
After all, running and arriving go hand in hand together.

This is a song, a sonnet you recite,
Whenever there's not much left inside.
You can cry, you can pray,
But what's yours will always make its way.

Renovations

When you finally let go,
Of all the dark things that were consuming you whole,
You actually see a world and a life that you make your own.

Like a house left abandoned, that had just been bought,
I am making a home with all the remnants of my past.
Trying to fix the broken thing, but not trying to change them,
Because they are proof, that one can always start brand new.

I am putting new pictures, and fixing old frames,
I'm learning how to breathe again.
I collecting the pieces of shattered glass and my heart,
And putting them in a box labelled art.

I've dusted the couched and the furniture,
Finally made my bed, woke up from a dark slumber.
Washed the dishes and the sins,
I let myself bathe in sunlight again.

Folded the laundry and the apologies,
Put them in the right places.
Held new hands and kissed good byes,
To all the empty faces.

Prayed again, a sign of hope,
I let my words be heard to whoever was willing to cope.
Wrote some line, beyond confines,
Added some happy times.

Arranged my records and my memories in order,
Played them and smiled over and over.
Brought new beginnings and forgiveness home,
Started healing from the things no one apologised for.

Sealed the cracks and the wounds,
But let them stay because they are alluring in their own ways.
Began accepting the chipped walls and scars all over,
Let myself have a do-over.

Smelled old books and read phrases divine,
Slowly-slowly and imperfectly my stars aligned.
Slept without guilt, let myself rebuild.
Constructed and reconstructed, altered life, let myself live
rather than just survive.

Painted new scenes and lit some candles,
This new glow felt good in my bones.
Will it last? No one knows.
But it has just made its way, and I'm willing to host it as long
as it will stay.
And if it decided to leave one fine day;
I'll pack its bags and let it go, I'll wave goodbye,
With no remorse.
And I'll wait, and be patient for it to show again.

But for now, I'll paint my walls and plant my daisies,
I'll raise a toast to being young and free.

Of Forgiveness and home

Forgiveness is something,
I gave away for free, I still do maybe,
But not when it comes to myself,
I beat myself up for every wrong, every false deed.
Every sorrow, every scene.

Hurt, pain, anger, whatever it was,
I hid behind doors, put them under a cloak.
With a smile so huge, that it dripped kindness and warm hues,
I gave away forgiveness,
Like candy and fruits.

I smiled, never cried,
I forgave them,
The world and all its consuming light.
Because I knew regrets more than I knew my own skin,
And I knew how guilt eats you from within.

So from my bag of kindness and love,
I picked forgiveness,
And sprinkled it around like fairy dust,
Left it in places that were forgotten and devoid of grace,
And decorated my house with bells that chimed,
Songs of love and rhymes unwind.

But wore gloves and covered in lace,
So none of that forgiveness could touch and trace.
Wore cover ups so that not even a speck,
Could land on my face.

Gave, never kept.
Left never received.
Touched never felt.
Kept never cherished.
Had but never devoured.
Smiled so hard,
That in the end all I could do was weep.

But no more,
For I'm forgiving myself
For all the sins and so much more.
I am done rubbing salt on open wounds.
Done stitching only for tearing.
Not letting this blood stain anymore furnishing.

Collecting all my dried flowers, dead long,
Putting them over caskets, where they belong.
No more digging, no more burials,
I am done holding lonely funerals.

So in fits and starts, and bits and pieces,
I'm learning to forgive myself
And all my weaknesses.
No more guilt, no more shame,
I am finally chasing them out the door.

The darkness is tiring,
And I'd like some light before retiring.
After all I'm not just skin and bones,
I am also a mind and a soul,
And I don't want to be adorned anymore.

Begin Anew

Too young, to pack so much.
Too young, to carry it around.
It's not something to be worn as a crown.

All this baggage, spilling over the rims,
A bottle thoroughly overfilled.
Of the clothing and the pictures,
Crammed and shut, thrown into the mixture.

The memories and more,
Of times lovely and lost.
And of times horrid at most.
All these words, stuck in the throat.

Songs that were ruined, by memories they inflicted,
Pictures that were tainted by ink splotches and tear droplets,
All the things that were packed, bottles sealed and left unsaid.
Finding ways to make an imprint,
To free themselves.

All this baggage that was never meant to be,
Weighing down all the happiness and possibilities.
No longer will I hold, all this and more,
No longer will I let more sorrow hoard,
All this space that was meant for smiles and light and all
things bright.

I rip open the bags and un-stuff, let go;
All the things I do not wish to hold anymore
All the pieces that I shouldn't have let pile more and more.
Letting go is sometimes tougher than it shows.

Took down the paintings, put them in memory lane,
Made space for new sceneries, and hope abundant.
I painted the walls a fresh white to collect mementos,
Not silent, unspoken struggles and fights.

And then I cleaned every nook, every cranny,
Wipe off the counters, removed the dead flowers,
And I left the doors and window ajar, for happiness and air and hope.
And wrote all those words that were haunting me,
Making me bleed, and at last I let myself finally weep.

When the tears had stopped and the air was no longer stale,
I threw all the decay out my home, and let myself finally pray.
To gods, that healed and to the gods that destroyed,
I prayed to the power and finally said,
I'm open, and will be from now,
This is my home not a junkyard, for memories, nightmares,
Dreams, reality, things, unspoken words, silence, lost love,
Broken things and predators to hound.

This is where I let go,
Let myself breathe, I'm done giving myself a hard time,
For every wrong deed.
Human, that's me,
Bound to break and make mistakes and breathe.

Forgive

Do the wounds ever heal?
The ones on surface you can't see?

All I did was learn to live,
With wounds that always bled over the brink.
Learned to stitch them with eyes closed,
And ripped them apart when the voices told to do so.

Rubbed salt, on these open gashes,
Made sure, they never closed all the way through,
Because pain was all I ever knew.
Let the cycle continue,
Of hurt and almost healing and pain and wounds new.

Took some time but realised at last,
My now is not my forever,
And nothing lasts.
Neither does the light nor the dark.

Learned forgiveness, took some time,
Because all this anger was pent up inside,
It was hard to let go of the endless fights.
Struggled but learned, that in the end it's yourself you've got,
Be gentle, this body, this home, this mind, this soul,
Shelters wonders beyond words.

Forgive yourself, for all the mistakes,
Be gentle, we all are trying.
Forgive the world, *I know you're angry at it,*
But let go, all this anger, let it go,
Forgive yourself, you're struggling I know.
Forgive yourself, it's okay to break and barrow.
Forgive yourself.
Forgive.

Poetry

I have light-years worth of poetry inside my head,
Banging its hands against my skull,
Scrambling, climbing, itching, trying to come out.
Finding ways to escape, to live, to be out and about,
To breathe this air, to end or maybe create more despair,
To be rid of this cage, this prison that captivates,
To be free of me, the worst enemy.

It screams and sings, it bleeds from within,
It cries at night, and burns like a fire bright,
It scratched and scratches, runs around in circles,
Ends up where it started, and repeats this cycle distorted.

I have light-years worth of poetry inside my heart,
Pumping with, the rhythms of the beat,
Coursing through my veins, side by side with blood together.
It seeps through wounds, in form of blood,
And through tears, when my heart hurts.
Looks for escapes everywhere, in every space,
Crams itself, wherever it can fit.
Pushes and pulls and every opening,
Spills like heavy linen on silk sheets.

It dances, it races,
It's loud and it leaves its traces,
It fights, flights,
Turns its back towards the light.
Falls to the ground, heavy like damp clothes,
Rests for some time, a grave its home,
Wakes again, births more,
It never really leaves me alone.

I have light-years worth of poetry inside my soul,
Blazing like a fire, burning like coal.
Heavy like branches after thunderstorms,
At times unbearable like war gore.
Soft like a tender kiss, warm like the graze of finger tips,
Black as the night, dark as the ink, red like wine,
Spilt on blank canvases.
Blooming like buds, wilting like flowers,
Decaying like bones turned to dust.
Rhythmic like music, jagged like broken glass,
Sweet like honey, bitter like a hollow laugh.

All these words, all this sorrow, flicks of happiness,
With pride that was swallowed.
All this dark looking for light,
And all this hope, waiting to take flight.
All the flowers wanting to bloom,
All this life trapped inside a tomb.
So I let it flow and let it out,
These words of grief and pain,
And paint them with light and fluttery hope,
And brace myself for what's next,
For I'll let these forever sing,
No more trapping what's within.

Questions They Ask

With their eyes open and hearts closed,
They ask me the following lines:

Do you even know the dark ?

Yes, yes I do, better than the morning hue.
I dip my fingers in it every now and then,
And dragged them across skin, bones, paper, walls
And hearts open.
I stain all the white so that there is no light
And I drink the rest, to ease what I cannot put to rest.

Do I even know the dark?
I know it better than my very own skin,
It has stayed with me when all the hope rotted within.
It gave me life, perhaps of irony, but a life still,
And it mended my broken soul, with dark cement and all things dead.
It stayed with me when people did no longer,
And it cried for staining me a deep haunting colour.

Do you even know heavy closed lids under the weighing mist?

I know and I understand, what it's like to have your eyes closed,
In broad daylight.
Empty but heavy,
Open yet closed,
Seeing not watching,
Looking never remembering.

Glazed over by thoughts of beyond,
And what if and what not.
Sheer nothingness, yet too much t o hold,
These eyes have a million stories,
Waiting to be told.

Do you even know longing and prison ?

Better than I know affectionate rhythms.
Chains familiar than any article of clothing,
Heavily wrapping this heart and these wrists.
Locked inside this unknown space,
It's a prison, right?
If you can't escape.

Do I know longing and cages?
Yes I do, I always feel like a captive,
In familiar places.
What's this body, if not a jail,
I cannot be rid of it until it's too late.

Do you even know light?

Not really, but I'm taking my time,
To understand the riddle it brings in its plight.
It hasn't been too long since I let it inside my life,
So treading unfamiliar territories, I'm accepting,
That the light that blinds also gives warmth time to time.

Do I even know light?
Not surely, but I'm learning,
I'm running my hands under unfiltered hues,
Staining my skin golden and blue.
I'm keeping it close, holding it in my fist,
I do not want to make friends with the dark again.

Do you even know hope?

I knew it once but I let go,
It was becoming a weapon more and more.
But only because I let it,
I let go of it when I should've kept it.
It ran away from me, to unknown places,
It slipped from my hands like sand between toes,
Washed over by grief and sorrow.

But here I am, making my way to it again,
After running in circles, I'm risking it again.
Restored by faith, in things and more,
I'm trying to finally make this strange land my humble abode.

Do you even know smiles?

I'm practising it again, anyways it's easier than frowning.
It is less exhausting than tears and brings joy.
It even makes my gloomy days bright,
Erases traces of haunting nights,
Not used to it, but giving it a try,
I'm feeling more and more alive.

Do I even know smiles?
All I know is that a stranger on the road gave it to me for free,
And it made me feel warm and sweet.
So I'm going to start returning the favour,
For I'm everyone's healing from things they once savored.

Do you even know yourself?
they ask at last, and I give them the most honest answer,
Simple and short.

Do I even know myself?
That I do not, but aren't I the part of the universe,
And the universe remains unknown,
We've made peace with not knowing the very space,
Why not make peace with not knowing ourselves too.
We are not a puzzle to be solved, a riddle put on hold,
You and me, we are our own celestial bodies,
No one, not even us will ever know it completely.

Progress

I walked down the road, and did not hide behind my clothes.
Take as little of space, That's progress I suppose.

Smaller and smaller,

Dim your light and paint your face.
Trim the ends, that hang loose,
And sway with wind wild and free.
Confine, this box is all you've got.

* * *

Made myself smaller, took littlest of space,
Felt guilty if I let my light own the stage.
Regretted speaking, got quiet,
Felt like a stranger in any attire.

Cut off pieces, to fit into even smaller spaces,
Hid behind clothes.
A human or a ghost?
Cried as soft as a whisper,
Felt like a nuisance when all I did was exist.
Footprints as sift and as unseen as mist,
Mastered the art of hiding in plain sight,
So still, it looked like a statue at times.

Built some walls, cemented them with tears and more,
Kept the world outside, missed out on many amazing times.
These walls grew thicker and thicker each day they were left to harden,
That at last I was left trapped in my own suffering.

Took some time, but finally took down the walls,
Peeled the plaster with my bare hands,
Scratched the concrete with my finger nails,
Bled and cried,
But in the end destroyed the monument of misery,
And let the grief flow, free and in waves,
Let it go wherever it wished to.

Let myself feel,
Destroyed the confines, let myself heal.
No more walls, just open windows,
And doors with welcome mats.
No more boxes, just free spaces,
And garden with blooms,
No more hiding,
Everything good and bad, out on display.

No more quiet,
Music and melodics,
And cries and screams,
No more whispers that haunt and lurk,
Just loud and clear words.
No more ghosts of me and things I can't control.
No more graves, no more lost hope.
Not more existing but living and living loud and proud.
No more regrets, just cherished moments,
No more running in circles, just healing and opening new doors.
No more apologies for taking space,
I'm here, I exist and I take space,
Space for all the love and words and feeling I hold,
Space for this body and this soul.

From Venom to Lights

Telling myself the nightmares don't last,
I was stuck with one regardless of that.

This body and this soul,
No more than a bad dream vivid and old.
I kept myself alive, telling myself,
You can't just give up the fight.

Twitching, touchy, sensitive,
Sweating in the midst of cold.
Year four, after my birth,
First time I felt so out of love,
With myself and this world.

The feeling left after a few knick-knacks,
But returned eventually only to last.
Skip-skip-skip year thirteen of this life,
First time I hysterically cried,
About this body and that it just doesn't suffice.

Years that came after,
Bought so much hate and disaster.
You are not supposed to hate your home,
But *I did, though.*
It haunted me, at days and at nights.
What kind of nightmare comes lurking in broad daylight?

I murdered things, martyred the four -year-old child,
I buried its body in plain sight.
Inside me, I let the flowers of dark bloom,
I let them contaminate every flower pristinely groomed.
And I buried more and more,
Made more graves, wrote more stones,
Dug some mud to bury beautiful things unknown.

At night, I usually cried, for all the battles I couldn't fight.
And all the things that I just let die.
And by the morning I let hate grow, and consume me whole.
Regrets and guilt gnawed and chewed on my now tainted soul.
Felt brokenness crack all my dreams and hopes.

So much hate, so much remorse,
Filled my veins with venom and remorse.
The gruesome things that I thought,
About myself and all that I've lost,
Had me choking, gasping and reaching for air.

Always submerged head deep in toxins and venoms,
Rotting my bones and all things that I still belovedly hold.
How much can one take before finally breaking?
How much of this am I taking?

Had nothing more to lose, so I finally let go,
Told myself that it's okay not to be okay.
And then preached myself the greatest of lines,
"Loving yourself and accepting yourself doesn't mean accepting
You're beautiful, but letting yourself exist regardless ."

This is a Lullaby

I'm writing this for you,
You brave-brave warrior.
Who's been fighting too long,
Who's been here, dusk till dawn.
Keep the sword down, take off the armour now.
For it's time to go home now.

Sip some water,
Close those eyes,
Now you may, stop the fight.
I'll weave your blankets
With lights and stars,
I'll make you a bed
Of wool and sweet songs,
I promise to keep the thunder out
And let them voices shut out

Shall you rest,
I'll go take care of this mess.
Don't you worry;
I will take care what's left.

You've done enough,
Fought many wars,
Once that can be seen
And the ones that cannot

Hands, calloused and rough,
For yielding the weapon you never wanted to pick up,
Your soul and your body sported wounds,
That you never once deserved.

I'll sew the cuts
With threads of healing
For them battle wounds
Left untreated.

I'll cover them up with gauzes of light,
So that when you wake up,
You can see the end of the night.

The battle wasn't supposed
To last this long,
But you see
Now it's over,
I'll take your armour and your sword,
And I'll hang it on the walls, you don't need them anymore.
I'll prepare you warm brews and steamy stews,
For you can relax and you can let go,
Of all this remorse you've held close.

I'll take your hand in mine
And whisper in your ear,
This sweet-sweet lullaby.

Hope and Growth

Late at night and I'm writing these words,
I'm up-up and up
And I feel more alive than ever before,
These words bubbling inside of me,
They're confined no more.

Earlier this week I read my old diary entries,
And realised how far I've reached.
The pages yellowed from time,
And in that messy scrawl were written,
Sad, sorrowful lines.
Now here I am, writing hope,
Never knew this day would come thru.

These words of mine are no less than a victory flag,
I made it, perhaps not unscathed,
But what's a war without battle scars.
I see my cursor blinking,
And all that's inside, is the warmth unfurling.

But there's always this thought looming my mind,
Lurking like a hand waiting to destroy.
What if it's all temporary and it won't last,
How will you survive another path so dark?

I answer myself like a scared child,
Who's learnt, life isn't always candies and sunshine.
I tell myself, that, like the dark this too, won't last,
But there will always be, a brighter path.

The warmth will perhaps, leave for a while,
But I will not let hope run away again,
I'll hold it close and cradle it in my hands,
I'm going to run my fingertips over its soft edges,
And wait till the black has eradicated.

For we are mere pawns in this game,
Ones of power and crimes,
Surviving on borrowed time.

I've learnt and I've cried,
Acceptance brings so much joy,
It's as liberating as letting go.

But I know that nothing shall last,
So like a child who carries its toy,
I carry my hope, everywhere I go.
For I've lived without and I know,
How hard it is to let certain things go.

These Words

I had to get over six layers of guilt, remorse,
Resentment, embarrassment, regret and denial,
To write these words.
But I wrote these because I should,
Because I fought my demons without any help,
And no one should feel that helpless.

So I wrote these words because what starts dark
Can always end in light,
Your now is not your forever,
Just remember the sun will once again shine.
And the grief and the sorrow and the pain will subside.

So written here on these pages,
Are all the words I couldn't speak,
And all the words that I wish
someone would have spoken to me,
So this me, right here telling you that it does get better,
And the cold leaves too,
The numbness after pain is a part of healing too.

Next time when you're falling apart,
And cannot think of life after dark,
I want you to open these pages,
And *read-read-read-read*,
The night, how it persisted,
But when the curtains were finally lifted,
The light that entered filled me with something unknowable,
And all my *sorrysorrysorry,* turned into songs uncanny.

So read and understand,
that I'm right here holding your hand.
And whispering in your ear
That this is not the end.

I hope these phrases knitted with love and care,
Will help you understand,
That there is an end to every despair.
Let go of the anchor that's not letting you float,
Just let go and hope.

* * *

All I wish is for these words to
give you hope and bring you home.
I hope you're home now.
This is where it ends but then again journey ends
only to begin again.

About the author

Sara Tripathi is a 17 year old high school student, poet and trained kathak performer. From a very young age Sara has taken a keen interest in writing, and has been an avid reader her whole life. Her days are spent reading and putting her thoughts into words. As much as she loves reading and writing, the same will always be her passion. She also loves spending her time painting colours on blank canvas and reading tarot, her love for art in any shape or form is incomprehensible. She believes that art is a medium so whole that it carries your expressions like no other. Writing and dancing are two things that she finds most solace in, she has given kathak performances on state as well as national platforms. What lies within, is Sara's first book, it's a collection of poems that will reach your heart and stir your soul, with this book the author wants to take you on an emotional journey of love, darkness, losing yourself but in the midst of all the chaos creating a home.

Sara may be reached at orphicwords2003@gmail.com or find her on Instagram with user id @orphicwords_

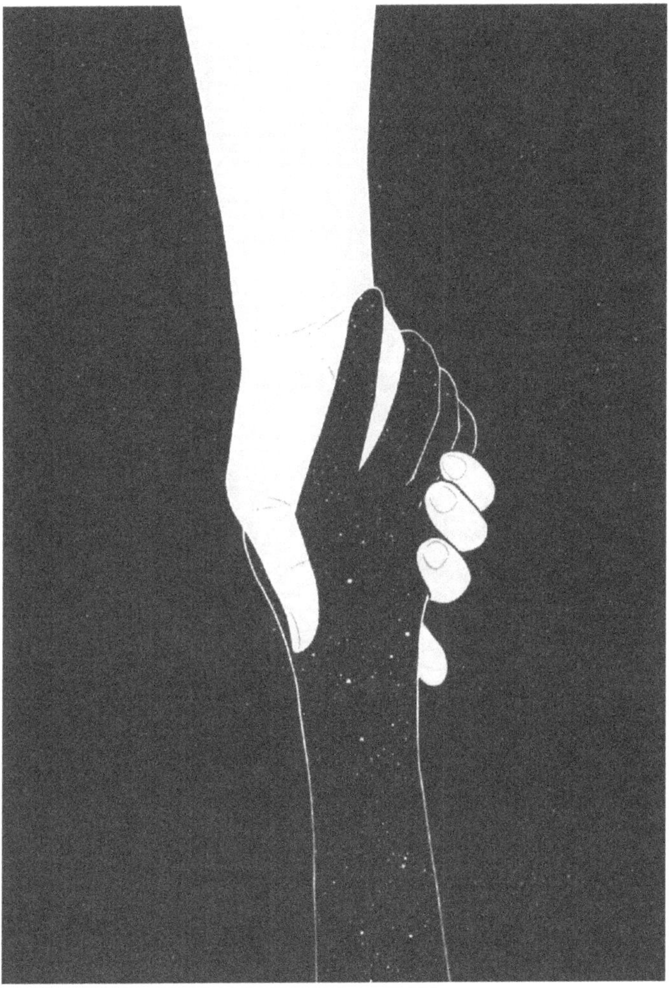